THE HOW AND WHY WONDER BOOK OF

BASIC INVENTIONS

Written by Irving Robbin
Illustrated by Leonard Vosburgh
Editorial Production: Donald D. Wolf

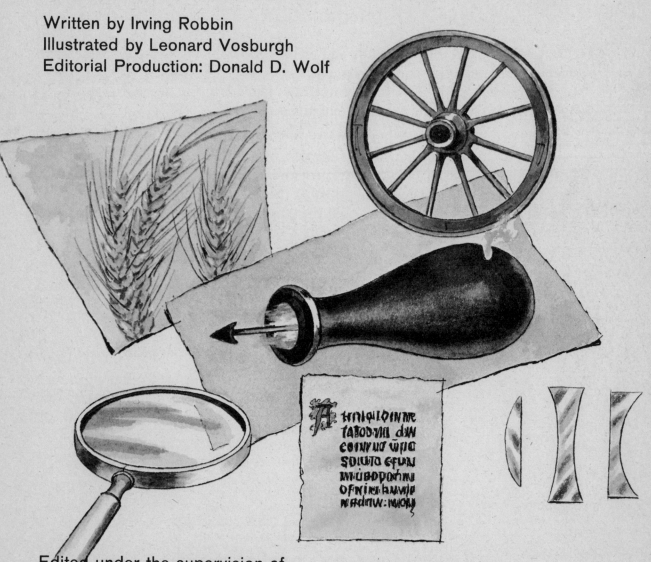

Edited under the supervision of
    Dr. Paul E. Blackwood, Washington, D. C.
Text and illustrations approved by
    Oakes A. White, Brooklyn Children's Museum, Brooklyn, New York

WONDER BOOKS · NEW YORK
A Division of GROSSET & DUNLAP, Inc.

Introduction

In these times when scientific and technological advances are so numerous, we may take for granted some of the basic inventions that have come to us from the past. This book forcefully reminds us of the heritage of discoveries we have received from our predecessors.

There is evidence that in every historical period men got along somehow with the familiar things that were available to them for satisfying their basic needs of food, clothing, and shelter, as well as their religious, social, and esthetic requirements. There was probably the same resistance to new inventions in the past as there is now, and there may have been long periods without any constructive change in the way man coped with his environment.

Yet, from time to time, there were tremendously significant discoveries and inventions which, as people accepted them, propelled civilization forward in great strides. Among these were the control of fire, the wheel, the microscope, the internal combustion engine, the telescope, controlled electricity, and the printing press — just to mention a few. Can you imagine the world without any one of these? What would your life be like without them?

This *How and Why Wonder Book of Basic Inventions* will stimulate an appreciation of man's ingenuity, and cause you to wonder what new inventions this century will bring. You can be sure there will be many. Who will invent them? It might be *you*.

Paul E. Blackwood

Dr. Blackwood is a professional employee in the U. S. Office of Education. This book was edited by him in his private capacity and no official support or endorsement by the Office of Education is intended or should be inferred.

Contents

Page

THE FIRST TOOLMAKERS   4

Why did man begin to invent things?   5
Do other creatures use tools?   6
Why is man's use of tools more
    important?   6
What are basic inventions?   7
What were the first basic inventions?   7

FIRE   7

How was fire discovered?   7
What were the first methods of
    making fire?   8
How does wood friction make fire?   10
What were the first uses of fire?   11
How did the discovery of fire lead
    to technology and industry?   11

AGRICULTURE   13

How were the principles of
    agriculture discovered?   14
When did cultivation of plants begin?   14
Where did formal agriculture first
    take place?   15
What were the first foods grown by
    man?   15
What were the changes wrought by
    the agricultural revolution?   15

THE WHEEL   18

Who invented the wheel and where?   18
What were the first steps in the
    development of the wheel?   19
What was the direct ancestor of the
    wheel?   20
What were the first uses of the
    wheeled vehicle?   21
Why is the wheel the most important
    mechanical invention?   22

GUNPOWDER   22

Who invented gunpowder?   23
How did the Europeans learn of
    gunpowder?   24
What were the first uses of
    gunpowder?   25

Page

What changes came about as
    the result of the invention of
    gunpowder?   26
Has gunpowder outlived its
    usefulness?   27

PRINTING   27

When did writing begin?   27
How was writing first used?   28
What were the next steps in the
    development of writing?   30
Who invented the alphabet?   30
What is movable type?   31
Who was the European inventor of
    printing?   32
What was the Gutenberg process?   33
What were the first books to be
    printed in this way?   34
What did the invention of printing
    mean to man?   34

OPTICS   35

Were lenses invented or discovered?   36
What was the practical use
    of the lens?   37
Did Galileo invent the telescope?   37
How was the telescope improved?   38
What is the importance of
    the telescope?   40
Who invented the microscope?   40
What science did the microscope
    revolutionize?   42
What was the first camera
    to use a lens?   42
To what other uses have lenses
    been put?   43

FROM THEN TILL NOW   44

The steam engine   44
Electricity   45
The internal combustion engine   45
Flight   46
Mass production   46
Long-distance communication   47
Atomic energy   47
Rockets and satellites   48

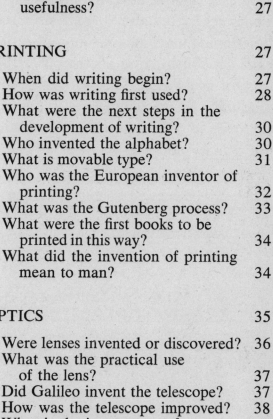

The First Toolmakers

There is no such thing as a complicated invention. There are complicated *machines,* but the basic ideas and devices that make up a complex mechanism are almost always fairly simple. The sleek, streamlined, and smoothly functioning machines of our civilization have developed from all the clever but simple inventions and discoveries that gradually accumulated over the many centuries of human history. Combining several simple, but basic, inventions and discoveries can result in a complicated machine such as the automobile, which could never have come about without the wheel, the process of smelting metals, electricity, and several other inventions and discoveries. That is what has happened throughout history.

True inventions are almost always uncomplicated. If they are not simple in concept, they can be expressed simply.

One of the first implements used by primitive man may have been a jawbone of an animal.

First row: Peking Man's tools (Old Stone Age, about 1,000,-000 B.C.).

Second row: Neanderthal Man's tools (Stone Age, about 50,000 B.C.).

Third row: Cro-Magnon Man's tools (New Stone Age, about 10,000 B.C.).

Just as a chimpanzee or other primate may pick up a natural object and use it as an implement, man's first implements most probably were the things he found and could use as extensions of his arms and hands; the jawbone of an animal could be used as an ax, or a stone picked up could be used as a hammer. Only much later did man discover that the stone could be shaped and made fit for different purposes. It is this ability to devise a tool for future use which creates one of the big distinctions between man using a tool and an animal using a chance implement.

Einstein's famous equation "$E = mc^2$," although the result of years of intense work, expresses the whole field of atomic energy. And what could be plainer than a wheel spinning on an axle? These are simple and basic ideas, yet they show the directness and purposefulness of man's inventive mind.

In the beginning, man never deliberately

Why did man begin to invent things?

set out to invent things. The devices that were first designed were accidentally discovered, or built because of need or the

The first fishhooks were made from shells.

desire to improve a hard life. The first inventions were simple tools — devices with which to cut, to hammer, to dig, or to throw — tools that, at first, were extensions of the hands. Later, much later, man's inventiveness extended to his eyes, ears, legs; eventually, he even learned to fly in machines. However, at the beginning, perhaps a million years ago, primitive man could only shape stones and sticks to give his already skillful hands added power.

There is a burrowing wasp (Ammophila) that uses a pebble, held in the mandible, to flatten the earth over the hole in which its eggs are hidden.

There is a finch (Cactospiza) that uses a cactus spine to pry insects from the tree bark.

There is a sea otter that uses a stone as a hammer to crush a shell.

A monkey uses a stick to get hold of a banana which fell outside his cage.

Do other creatures use tools? Man was not the first of the creatures on earth to use a tool. There is a burrowing wasp that uses a pebble for a tamper to pound the sand down over her nest. A finch that lives in the Galapagos Islands pries insects from the crevices in tree trunks with a cactus-spine lever, and the English spotted woodpecker holds open a cleft in a tree branch with a pine-cone wedge. The sea otter, while floating on its back in the water, is known to place a stone on its chest and hammer a shellfish on it until the shell breaks open. And finally, many of the monkeys and apes sometimes use sticks and stones as levers and missiles.

Why is man's use of tools more important? The great difference between man and the tool-using animals is that while animals follow an inherited instinctive pattern, a manner of behavior that if it varies at all does so only slightly from generation to generation, man can learn. Also, animals use only those tools they find that fit the purpose. Man builds his! Man has a conscious concept of a tool's use and makes a conscious effort to design one that will do the job. In addition to building tools, man seeks to improve them.

In the prehistoric days, early man deliberately chipped pieces of stone until he had a hammer head or a cutting edge. He sharpened the ends of sticks for spears, and lashed handles to his stone tools. He wove grasses together to form mats, and learned to make fire.

Man began to consciously invent devices that would make life easier for him, devices to protect him, devices to entertain him. Man was never content to accept just what the environment of the world around him offered. He, even now, constantly seeks to change it, to control it, to make it serve him. This is how he became an inventor.

For hundreds of millions of years, the animals endured their way of life on earth and still do, but in the short 1,000,000-odd years that man has inhabited earth, he has literally changed his very relationship with the planet.

Man has made thousands of inventions,

What are basic inventions? but only several dozen are really basic. Basic inventions are those that lead to a change in the manner of man's life on earth. It is one thing to invent a better hammer, but it is completely different and more important to invent a wheel or gunpowder. Inventions like these changed the direction of progress and led humanity into new paths.

The first devices that were truly impor-

What were the first basic inventions? tant and that set man on the path to civilization were simple hand tools and weapons. They were all made of wood, stone, or bone, materials early man could find and shape to his needs. However, they served to start him on the long road of technology and culture. The primitive hammers, scrapers, spear points, and stone knives were only the beginning. There was much more to come.

Fire

Man did not invent fire. He discovered how to use it. This single discovery did more to raise him above an animal existence than any other invention or discovery. Fire was the first force that gave man some independence of his environment. It became the basis for the vast amount of technology that followed in the years to come, and is still the basis for most of our modern technical processes.

Fire is a natural phenomenon and oc-

How was fire discovered? curs in nature quite often. The eruption of volcanoes, the spontaneous combustion of decaying matter, and bolts of lightning all produce natural fires. Primitive man, living completely in the wilds, was in a good position to observe such production of fire. He also observed its effect — destruction. But at the same time, he must

When man first dared to "steal fire from the gods," he had to keep it burning as he did not know how to make it himself.

Once early man had captured a bit of fire, perhaps a burning stick from a forest fire, he kept it going by adding small bits of wood from time to time.

have noticed that fire gave light and warmth, and so he set about to tame the flaming demon in order to use its good qualities. He regarded fire as a demon because it seemed to be alive and because it consumed many things. After all, the ability to move and to eat are signs of life. Natural fire does both these things with a majestic and uncontrolled power. For these reasons, primitive man made fire one of his gods, but at the same time he realized that, by rationing the fuel, he could make that god work for him.

A fire that is carefully fed with a small amount of fuel is a controlled fire.

In the beginning, man did not know how to make **What were the first** fire, so he **methods of making fire?** stole it from nature's own fires. When he moved from place to place, he had to carefully carry and preserve the glowing coals for if they went out, he would have to wait until nature provided him with another supply. But he finally learned how to make it for himself.

Evidences of man-made fire are still being discovered as scientists dig deeper and deeper into man's past. They discovered that the men who lived during

At left and above, the primitive and cumbersome methods of making fire, a discovery which started man on the road to civilization.

the geologic era known as the Pliocene used fire. This dates all the way back to 250,000 years ago, the time when Peking Man lived. Peking Man is one of the oldest in the ancestral history of our race. He received his name because his remains were first found in a limestone cave near Peking, China. Within this cave were also the charred ashes of wood and bone that indicated that Peking Man used fire as part of his domestic life.

No one yet knows just when men be-

gan to make fire themselves, but scientists believe that it happened very early in history. They say that it must have come about as a result of the observation of sparks. Forest fires are spread by hot sparks blown by the wind, and the early toolmakers must have noticed that the rocks they chipped at often threw off similar sparks. Following up on this observation, these first artisans obviously began to select those rocks that would make sparks every time they were struck. A very common mineral, iron pyrites, will give a shower of sparks when hit with another stone, and flint, the basis for many early tools, will do even better.

This method of producing sparks by striking stones together is known as percussion, and all that is needed to start a fire is to direct the sparks to a pile of tinder made of dry leaves and tiny scraps of wood. Later on, much later, the combination of iron and flint became standard in the production of sparks. It was used in early rifles, and is still used by some primitive peoples.

The other system of fire-making that was developed in primitive time is that of wood-friction. Many methods and devices have been invented to produce fire by rubbing wood together. Some are quite simple. The fire-saw consisted of a serrated block of wood; another piece was rapidly scraped back and forth across the toothed edges. The fire-plough was made in roughly the same way, with a grooved piece of wood and another piece that was slid rapidly back and forth in the groove.

The most successful of these was the fire-drill. This device consisted of a block of wood with a hole partially cut into it. A stick with a rounded end was inserted into the hole and rotated rapidly. There were many variations in the method of rotation. In some, the stick was spun between the hands; in others, a twisted cord was used to create the rotation. Perhaps the most successful of all fire-drills was the one that used a bowstring in tension. All the fire-maker had to do was twist the string over the stick and move the bow rapidly.

But it did not matter what method was employed. The important thing was that they all produced fire.

Obviously, if one rubs two pieces of wood together rapidly, they will become quite hot.

How does wood friction make fire?

The common belief is that this heat eventually ignites the wood and the fire-maker is successful. But there are two things wrong with this assumption. First, if the wood did ignite and begin to burn, the fire-maker would be successful, but he would lose his tool and have to build a new one each time he needed a fire. Second, it is very rare that a thick piece of wood will start burning just from friction. It may char, but a blaze is what is really desired.

The success of a wood-friction fire device is due to the wood dust that is scraped off by the movement. The basic requirement is that one piece of wood be harder than the other so that it acts like a file or a sander. Then there must be a groove or hole — in effect, a little oven — within which the scrapings can accumulate. As the drill is rotated, or the stick slid back and forth, it sands off tiny shavings from the block, known as the hearth. These collect in the hole or groove, which becomes hotter and hotter as the friction warms the entire area. Since the shavings and wood dust are so small, they absorb the heat rapidly and soon begin to blow. A tiny puff of air will make them burst into flame and they can be shaken out and onto a pile of tinder. The result of these efforts: a fire!

Early man found several very important uses for fire.

**What were the
first uses of fire?**

The first was as
heat. Not being
equipped with protective fur, man found
fire extremely useful during the long
cold winter nights. Built under the shelter of a rock overhang, or inside a cave,
a fire gave a cozy warmth. However, it
also produced light, and light gave
more meaning to the long dark nights.
It was probably by firelight that the
first artists in history painted the wonderful pictures which have been found
in prehistoric caves. This light also enabled the women to make clothes, and
the men to chip their weapons. It shut
out the cold and darkness and created,
for the first time in history, a home for
a family.

Fire performed another valuable
function as well. All wild animals, in-
cluding those that were dangerous to
man, were deathly afraid of the blazing
heat which singed fur and caused pain
and death. So fire was perhaps man's
first defensive weapon. But there were
other and more important uses of fire
yet to come.

It seems quite natural today to use
fire to supply the heat needed to cook
food, but it undoubtedly took a great
many years before early man learned
to use fire in that way. Perhaps it came
about accidentally when some raw meat
fell into a fire, or maybe hunters found
the burned bodies of animals after a
forest fire. Whatever the method of discovery, the use of fire for cooking was
extremely important in the history of
man.

There were two discoveries that must

**How did the discovery
of fire lead to tech-
nology and industry?**

have been
made right
after the first
domestic use
of fire. These were baking clay and
smelting metals through the use of heat.
Again, the discoveries were accidental.

As we do today when camping, primitive man heaped rocks around his fire
to contain it. It is thought that he must
also have used clay to hold the rocks in
position. Imagine his surprise when he
discovered that the clay became hard
after exposure to the heat! This was
actually the birth of the pottery industry, for it did not take inventive man
long to realize that, with his hands, he
could fashion useful shapes of the soft
clay and bake them into permanent
utensils and dishes.

Possibly at the same time, the heat
of the fire must have melted the metallic ores present in some of the stones,
and primitive man was treated to the
sight of molten metal pouring in tiny
rivulets from the red hot stones. When
the fiery little rivers hardened, he found
that he had a material that made better
tools and weapons than he had ever
had before. This first metal to be used
by primitive man was copper, easily
melted and easily shaped. He learned to
find the stones carrying the blue-green
trace of copper, melted the ore free of
the stone matrix, and poured it into
molds. Soon, he began to search for
rocks that contained other metallic ores.
It was a great step forward. Many thousands of years later when the iron age
was born, it was all because man had

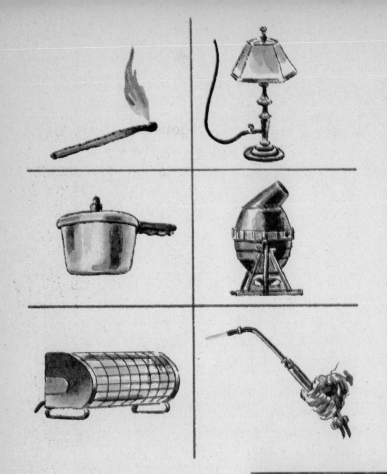

discovered how to tame "the fire god" and put it to work.

Man's use of fire has never ended. Today, we have many sophisticated methods of producing this natural phenomenon, but we still use fire in the same ways as primitive man when we cook, bake pottery, or smelt metal with it. We burn gas or oil to heat our homes and we use the hot electrically produced sparks to ignite the fuel in a gasoline or diesel engine. We are also finally learning to harness the heat of the hottest "fire" of all, the sun, to perform many more useful tasks.

Fire was one of the very first important discoveries that humans made. It is still one of the most important.

It is far cry from the making of fire with the fireplow to the striking of a match; from the lighting of the cave to see well enough to make the now-famous cave paintings to even the gas lamp which lit rooms not too long ago; from the roasting of a deer over an open fire to the use of the pressure cooker; from the crude forms of pottery and the smelting of ores to our modern clay ovens and Bessemer converters that manufacture iron and steel; from the heating of the cave with a wood fire to our furnaces and electrical heating appliances; from the frightening-away of an animal by a burning branch to the use of an acetylene blowtorch; but it all started quite accidentally when the first man dared to steal the first fire, the "secret of the gods."

Agriculture

Every living organism needs a continuous supply of food. It is one of the basic requirements of life. Trees and plants stand firmly rooted in the ground and soak up their nourishment, using the sunlight to create the necessary chemical changes. The herbivorous, or plant-eating, animals roam the forests and fields searching for the special kinds of vegetation they require. The carnivorous, or meat-eating, animals hunt other animals, tracking them through the underbrush and open prairies.

When man made his appearance on earth, he faced the same problem —

the need for a continuous supply of food — but he had an advantage, a biological advantage. A human being is omnivorous, meaning that he can digest many different kinds of food, vegetables as well as meat. In primitive times, man hunted almost exclusively, chasing and trapping animals and then cooking the meat. But at some time in his early history, he discovered that he could also eat certain plants and fruits. This must have been a momentous discovery, because hunting was a dangerous occupation, and the gathering of edible plants was a much more peaceful and safer way to fill the larder.

But there never were enough plants to last a season and none, of course, in the winter; the tribes had to move on, chasing game, finding untouched areas of vegetation. Life must have been a game of steady movement, a constant search for food, a competition with all the other forms of life.

Then came a great discovery, a method by which a supply of food could be grown in the same place year after year. Like other basic inventions and discoveries, this made a profound change in the life and development of man. Although some primitive tribes had already solved the problems of domesticating animals and raising them for food, this discovery was even greater. It was based on the knowledge that the seeds of plants could be gathered, saved through the winter, and placed in the ground the following spring. Then, after some months, a new supply of food was available.

No one knows how primitive man first

How were the principles of agriculture discovered? found out that seeds, if planted, would grow into plants. However, scientists have several theories. The most important is that of accidental observation. Although the early tribes were wanderers, they roamed a general area and obviously revisited the same places often. It is even likely that they had special camping places for the different seasons of the year. At the mouths of the caves and the edges of their campsites were the refuse piles where garbage and bones were tossed. Imagine the excitement of a sharp-eyed Stone Age man when he discovered that the shoots of plants were growing from the refuse piles! This discovery must have been made many times over in those early days of mankind, especially when a tribe returned to its spring campsite or to its winter caves.

But this was not the entire discovery. There was another step man had yet to take. He still had to find out *why* the plants were growing in his garbage heaps. This, too, was a matter of observation. Plant and fruit seeds, nuts, and pieces of edible roots were all part of the garbage, the remnants of the vegetation that the food-gatherers had brought in for meals. A careful examination showed the men of those times that the plants had obviously sprouted from the various seeds and roots. It could also be observed that new fruit trees always sprang up around the older ones, and a little digging at the roots of the young sprouts must have revealed the presence of seeds.

By making all these observations, primitive man made his discovery of agriculture complete. The next step was for man to put this discovery to work for him by deliberately cultivating the plants that provided food. This was the revolutionary step, the truly inventive idea, the mark of progress.

There is no definite date, just a general period when

When did cultivation of plants begin? agricultural cultivation is supposed to have started. It is now believed to have all begun some ten or twelve thousand years ago, a period known as the Neolithic Revolution, or the New Stone Age. The discovery of controlled agriculture was the second great change in the relation of man to environment (the first, you remember, came with fire), and it ushered in what is now called the Modern period.

There was a great deal to learn about growing plants for food, and it must have taken several thousand years of experiment before any kind of system was evolved. Men had to discover how to collect seeds, how to store them through the winter, and how to cultivate those plants which came up as perennials (continuing to live from year to year) by themselves. Also, much had to be learned about the land's preparation, fertilization, and irrigation.

However, the enterprising and inventive people of the Neolithic Age did teach themselves the skills necessary for the cultivation of plants for they changed their entire society from one of wandering hunters and herders to become the world's first farmers.

14

GOURD VESSELS

PRIMITIVE SPINDLE

Where did formal agriculture first take place? Scientists now definitely believe that the first formal farming of land began in the Middle East on the slopes of the Zagros Mountains in Kurdistan. In this area, archaeologists have found the earliest types of farm implements known as well as dried kernels of wheat and other seeds. Wooden and stone plowshares, stone dishes, and other devices to grind grain were also discovered in this area. To be sure, similar discoveries have been made in other places in the Old World, and even in the New World, but modern dating methods prove that the Middle Eastern site is the oldest.

There is evidence, too, of permanent settlements in this part of Kurdistan, which shows that villages sprang up around the farming fields. These early people also had domesticated animals for food and labor. Of course, formal agriculture had also begun in many other places, even before the Kurdistan group, but it was haphazard and experimental. At this particular site was found the remains of the first formal farms in the entire history of man.

What were the first foods grown by man? The green vegetables were undoubtedly the first foods to be cultivated by the early farmers. They were the easiest to grow. Lettuce, spinach, and cabbage led the way, to be followed by the cereal plants. Two types of early wheat, einkorn and emmer, appeared very early in history, but barley, rye, oats, and millet were also cultivated.

At the same time, man began to gather nuts and fruit and to plant the trees that bore this produce, but he also cultivated plants for reasons other than food. Flax was grown to provide fibres for spinning and weaving, and cotton and hemp appeared for the same reasons. Gourds were cultivated to provide vessels for storing liquids, and plants and trees with broad leaves, like the palm and the date, gave men the materials with which to cover his roofs and weave his mats. The trees themselves gave wood for construction.

Taken as a whole, the controlled cultivation of plants initiated a completely new era for man.

What were the changes wrought by the agricultural revolution? The changes were many and basic. Man was no longer a wanderer following the migratory habits of the animals, risking his life in the chase. He now remained in the same place, perhaps for many generations, built a permanent home, and became a neighbor to his fellows instead of a tribal competitor. Once settled, he created communal meeting places, villages, and cities, where he could bring the produce of the land to trade for the work of artisans who made implements and farming tools. It was a new type of culture for the former wanderers, a life that kept him in closer contact with his fellows.

With the rise of the cities and their concentration of people, a form of government was required. The free-swinging days of tribal lawlessness had to give

EARLY EGYPTIAN USING PRIMITIVE SPINDLE

way to a set of rigid rules and laws that governed the conduct of the people. Although these early governments were fierce and tyrannical and often unfair, they were the beginnings of mankind's attempts at self-rule, the desire to set up a code of world behavior, a drive to rise from the "eat-or-be-eaten" life of the animals.

With man now adjusted to the rhythmic swing of the seasons, the sowing of the seeds, the tending of the plants, the reaping of the crops, and the storing of the food, man's religions changed. The old tribal gods were fierce and impersonal. The only time they took notice of man was to destroy him. These beliefs slowly gave way. Neolithic man never fully understood the miraculous mysteries of germination and growth.

He believed that they were all controlled separately, so he adapted his religion to conform with the earth cycle of farming. He went through elaborate planting rituals in the spring, harvest festivals, and winter rites — all planned to appeal to and appease the gods he thought controlled his food supply. The change was significant. Man now had gods that were directly interested in his welfare, that noticed him, that rewarded and punished in a more just manner. At first, there were many gods but slowly, over thousands of years, the belief in one God evolved which today is the basis of almost every major world religion.

There was another change in the basic life of man with his development of agriculture. As the cities increased

When man first became food-producer instead of food-gatherer, his tools were primitive. Digging sticks and rakes were used to loosen the ground, primitive plows were moved by man power (often woman power), and harvesting implements were often made out of baked clay. With the domestication of animals, man power was replaced by animal power and irrigation made the ground more productive.

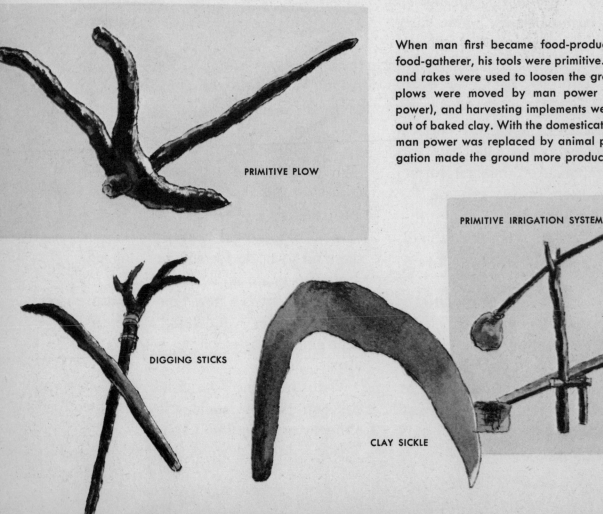

PRIMITIVE PLOW

DIGGING STICKS

CLAY SICKLE

PRIMITIVE IRRIGATION SYSTEM

in size and became filled with people who were not food-producers, the need for a larger food supply arose. Farms had to be extended and new lands prepared for the plow. Inevitably, this expansion led to conflict with neighboring cities that were expanding on their own. The cities became city-states — in some cases, countries — at war with each other. The fights were almost always over the control of more farming land.

Eventually, this turmoil resulted in the combination of cities and countries into empires that controlled thousands of square miles of the ancient world. This produced a new food problem. The empires required large armies for defense, thousands of men who did not produce food but who still had to be fed. And so the farmers spread out even farther.

The discovery of agriculture at first settled man, then made him organize his life with laws and religion, and finally, turned him against himself in war. The far-wandering hunter became the settled tiller of the soil, a community dweller, and a seeker of progress.

Our involved civilization of today actually began with agriculture — a civilization that learned to grow food efficiently and scientifically; a civilization that produced technology, art, and music; a civilization which, despite progress, is still struggling with the problems that began some ten thousand years ago with the appearance of the first farms.

While in underprivileged countries farming is very often done with tools only slightly improved over primitive ones, the mechanization of farm equipment in other parts of the globe helped greatly to feed the overpopulated world.

The Wheel

A wheel spinning on an axle seems a simple device, yet it is probably one of the most sophisticated inventions ever wrought. It was not only clever, it was also completely revolutionary. Almost every invention duplicates some function or process that happens in nature. Our eyes contain lenses and movable irises, and are in effect a sort of camera. Levers and pivots exist in our bodies. The intricate plumbing system through which our blood flows is controlled by valves and powered by a strong pump, the heart. Electricity occurs in many forms — the powerful displays of lightning; the storage of current in the organs of some sea creatures; the minute currents that travel along our nerves to stimulate the muscles. All kinds of chemical processes abound in nature from the slow crystalline workings of the earth minerals to the rapid changes in plants and animals. Atomic transformations occur constantly in the universe, within the hot, whirling inferno of a star, for example. It would seem as though everything man has made has been preceded by nature.

But nowhere in the universe, as far as we know, is there a wheel that spins freely on an axle. This is a device that man invented. It is his mechanical contribution to the universe, a concept that did not exist until he made his appearance. It may well be that the wheel will remain man's only original invention, the one device that does not duplicate something in nature.

Who invented the wheel and where? No one knows who invented the wheel. It is an invention that arrived gradually, step by step, over a long period of time — the result of the work of many men, many cultures, and many experiments. It was, therefore, not a spark of genius in the mind of a single inventor, but the result of centuries of work by a number of inventors that led to the greater mobility of man.

The wheel appeared in many places and in many forms in the lands surrounding the Mediterranean Sea. It is not very old if we use the entire history of humanity as a time scale. The first true wheels appeared no more than five or six thousand years ago and spread rapidly from wherever they were built throughout the ancient world.

It is fascinating to study the development of man's technological progress in terms of the wheel. It is believed that man became a tool user some 1,000,000 years ago and that thousands of thousands of years went by until he made a wheel. But consider the progress that has been made in the relatively short space of time, 6,000 years, since the wheel was invented. It is a phenomenal rate of speed — 6,000 years against almost 1,000,000 — and shows how truly important the wheel was, and still is, to the growth of man's technology.

The first primitive wheels were found in the remains of Assyrian, Babylonian, and Egyptian cultures, and it possibly was invented simultaneously in those areas. However, we do know that it was never invented in the New World. The invading Spanish in the 16th century, bent on colonizing the continents of the Western Hemisphere, found the early American cultures quite advanced, but not one had a true wheel.

Scientists who have made a study of the origins of man's technology believe that the wheel was first

What were the first steps in the development of the wheel?

thought of as a result of the observation of partial rotary motion in the human and animal bodies. Our arms, legs, hips, shoulders, wrists, ankles, and even heads rotate to some extent but, of course, cannot turn all the way around. Early man, possibly noticing this semi-rotation, applied the principle to his fire-making. The wooden rod, spun by a bowstring, exhibits one of the first forms of man-made rotary motion. It is not complete rotary motion because the rod must spin in the opposite direction when the bowstring reaches the end of its travels. What was needed was a device that would go around continuously in the same direction.

The first real step toward this type of operation came with the development of the pivoted door. There were no hinges in those very ancient times, and the doors of houses were pivoted by means of pegs at top and bottom that turned in sockets in the door frame. Such sockets have been found in the ancient Assyrian ruins, some dating back to 4500 B.C. They were also found in areas around the Aegean Sea and in parts of Central Europe. All were from about the same period.

SUMERIAN CRAFTSMAN BORING STONE VESSEL

PIVOTING DOOR

THE POTTER'S WHEEL

CLAY TOY CART WITH DRIVER AND OXEN FOUND IN THE INDUS VALLEY.

TOY HORSE ON WHEELS FOUND IN AN EGYPTIAN BURIAL TOMB OF A CHILD.

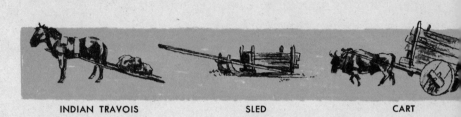

INDIAN TRAVOIS   SLED   CART

While primitive man may have made use of logs to move heavy objects, the development of the carriage could have gone from travois over sled to cart and four-wheeled carriage.

SUMERIAN WHEEL

GALLIC
WHEEL

ROMAN
WHEEL

DA VINCI
WHEEL

The Italian painter and inventor Leonardo da Vinci improved the wheel in the late 15th century by making it lighter and stronger.

This idea — a peg rotating in a socket — was not far removed from the concept of the wheel itself.

The use of rotating door sockets led to the potter's wheel. The potter's wheel was initially a circular disc of stone with a rounded hump on the bottom which was nested in a cup-shaped depression in another stone. When properly balanced and greased with animal fat, it could be spun quite easily. This was perhaps the first device that exhibited true, continuous rotary motion. Remnants of this type of primitive rotating machine have been found in the ruins of almost every early culture in the world. The ancient Greeks, Egyptians, Sumerians, and the Oriental groups all used various versions of this socketed potter's wheel.

What was the direct ancestor of the wheel?

Although the potter's wheel was not a true wheel, a device spinning freely on an axle, it was the last step along the line. All that was needed was to turn it on edge, bore a hole through the center, and spin it on a horizontal rod or axle. This was done some time between 3,000 and 4,000 years B.C. in many places in the ancient world. However, some method was needed to hold the wheel in place, and so the first hub caps were pegs driven through the wooden axle to prevent the wheel from sliding off.

The first wheels were made of wood, but not of one piece. Since it was difficult to obtain slabs of wood large enough to carve the circular shape of the wheel, ancient artisans nailed three pie-shaped segments together to form a circle. Since the wood wore out rapidly, a tire was needed to fit over the circumference and these, as first developed in Ur and Assyria, were originally made of leather and then bands of copper.

Once this spinning wheel was installed on vehicles, it made a quick and revolutionary change in man's habits.

20

FOUR-WHEELED CARRIAGE

At right, a Sumerian war char-
iot, one of the first uses of
the wheel.

Historians tell us that the first wheeled vehicles were war chariots.

What were the first uses of the wheeled vehicle?

The Sumerians, in 3500 B.C., swept across the pastoral world in their lumbering chariots, defeating all who crossed their path. Although they created a new and decisive style of warfare, their power did not last too long. Other groups also built horse-drawn chariots and adopted the new system of wheeled attack. The simple life of the ancient world was rapidly altered. An army on wheels could control a larger area, and soon, many conquered areas were consolidated into countries.

Many inventions throughout the history of man have resulted in a greater war potential, but they have also done much good in peaceful ways. The wheeled vehicle became a boon to the farmer. Their crude sleds were converted into wagons which the oxen could pull much more easily. The farmer's cart or wagon was a simple device, but it helped to create cities. With the overland transport of produce a much easier task, central markets sprang up in the villages. These markets became trading places for all sorts of merchandise, and the focal points for the growth of cities. In these centers, ideas as well as produce were exchanged, and the small world of five or six thousand years ago began to broaden in many ways.

Migration from place to place became simpler. People who wished to move to another area could carry their possessions, piled high in the primitive wagons, with them. The laboring oxen pulling steadily forward, the families looked ahead with anticipation to the new lands they were to live in.

It is safe to say that all of man's technology has either developed from the wheel or depends on its use in some form.

Why is the wheel the most important mechanical invention?

Just think of the many pieces of machinery that use wheels or were made with other machines that use wheels. The printing press that stamped the words on this page has many wheels within it, and the tiny gears in a wristwatch are a kind of wheel. Pulleys are wheels which can transfer power to other pulleys by means of belts. The armature in a generator is a wheel which gives us electricity, and our vehicles roll comfortably on our broad highways on smoothly running, rubber-tired wheels, which are powered by engines that have many wheels inside. Even motor boat engines have internal wheels, just like the automobile engine, and the propellor which thrashes the water into motion is another wheel. There seems to be no limit to the use of the wheel, but no matter how complicated and involved the machinery that uses wheels becomes, the wheel itself remains unchanged. It is still, in essence, a circular disc freely rotating on an axle.

Gunpowder

Having the knowledge of fire-making, metal-smelting, controlled agriculture, and that marvelous device, the wheel, mankind was able to go a long way. During the thousands of years before the birth of Christ, empires rose and fell, cities became more complex, and explorers began to probe into the unknown parts of the world.

Inventive men created machines to make work easier, faster, and more efficient. Archimedes of Greece in the third century B.C. worked out a water pump which used a hollow rotating screw. He designed the first workable pulley, and described the principle of the lever. A century later, Hero of Alexandria built a piston pump, a steam-operated sphere, and a siphon. From far-off China, in A.D. 105, came paper.

These inventions, and many others, were important but they were not basic. They did not point the development of civilization in a new direction. They were only clever new methods of doing age-old jobs more easily. None of them were as revolutionary as the wheel. In fact, many of these devices used the wheel as a basis for operation. The world had to wait a very long time for another truly basic invention.

Following the birth of Christ, the Roman Empire began a slow disintegration. Its far-flung edges were being nibbled away by barbarian tribes and, by A.D. 476, the Roman Empire had vanished as a major political force. The world now fell into the Dark Ages, a period of feudalism, ignorance, and despotism during which very little was accomplished. Inventions were few and far between, knowledge remained locked in the ancient books, people huddled within walled cities. Progress came almost to a standstill. But about 1,000 years after the birth of Christ, a new, and literally earthshaking, invention appeared — gunpowder.

No one knows who first mixed the chemicals that make up **Who invented gunpowder?** gunpowder. All that is known is that gunpowder was undoubtedly first made in China, and the earliest mention of the formula — a combination of potassium nitrate (saltpeter), sulphur, and carbon — is to be found in a Chinese book that was written in A.D. 1044. It is entirely possible that the Chinese

Berthold Schwarz experimenting with explosives.

It is very likely that the discovery of gunpowder happened accidentally in China, as the Chinese had developed fireworks displays long before the birth of Christ.

were using gunpowder long before this time. They were experts in the manufacture of fireworks, and great experimenters with chemical combinations that produced dazzling colors and powered skyrockets. Undoubtedly, there was fierce competition between fireworks designers, each having his own secret formulas and keeping his secrets well. Therefore, it is possible that one of the early Chinese chemists had discovered the gunpowder formula long before it was mentioned in 1044.

Just as the Battle of Agincourt on October 25, 1415, between the French and the English proved that the heavily armored French knights were no longer a match for foot soldiers and that the longbow outclassed the arbalest (crossbow), so proved the invention of firearms far superior to any kind of bow and arrow.

ARBALEST

How did the Europeans learn of gunpowder?

As the Dark Ages drew to a close, there was increasing overland travel to the Far East. Merchants began sending caravans over the long, dusty roads that wound their way through the Middle East, over the mountains, and into China and India. These traders must have brought back samples of the explosive compound.

However, European researchers were also working on the manufacture of gunpowder. In the 13th century, Roger Bacon, an English friar, mixed an explosive formula which is believed to have been gunpowder. Bacon did not try to find a use for his compound but only experimented with it as a curiosity. In the same century, saltpeter was mentioned in the writings of two other researchers as possessing fine incendiary properties. It may be possible that the Europeans were finding their own way to the manufacture of gunpowder. No one will ever know the true facts.

There is one incident, well-recorded in history, that points to the use of gunpowder in the Middle Ages. In the 14th century, a German monk, Berthold

Schwarz, mixed some chemicals together which blew up part of the monastery and himself, as well. Many historians believe that he, like the Chinese, discovered the proper proportions of saltpeter, sulphur, and carbon. Again, this is a fact that will never be proven. The evidence was blown to smithereens!

Whatever the origin, it was evident to the researchers of the Middle Ages that they had a new and powerful device. What they did not know was that gunpowder would shape the future history of humanity.

It is obvious that the first use of gunpowder would be in a weapon. It is an unfortunate comment on man that many of his fine inventions were first used for destruction. In the case of gunpowder, this is still its most important use. At the time gunpowder began to be used, the arbalest, or crossbow, was the most powerful weapon, but it needed a strong arm to wind up the spring. Gunpowder never needs winding up; it is always ready to explode with just a spark.

What were the first uses of gunpowder?

The initial use of gunpowder in a weapon was with the Arabian cannon known as a *madfaa*. This device, invented in the 1300's, was a thick wooden pot, filled with gunpowder, with a

The *pot de fer* was an improvement of the *madfaa*, the earliest known "cannon."

The use of gunpowder and guns played an important role in the success of the Spanish conquests in the New World.

25

round stone covering the opening at the top. A small touch-hole at the side permitted the insertion of a flaming match to ignite the charge. The Europeans improved on this with the *pot de fer,* an iron vessel shaped like a wine bottle and loaded with a tight-fitting iron arrow for a missile.

From these simple beginnings, firearms and cannons — all using gunpowder as the propellant force—developed rapidly.

The most immediate and widespread change came in the method of battle. Since firearms could strike objects at greater distances than arrows, hand-to-hand fighting diminished. Cannons could hurl either solid or gunpowder-filled shells that destroyed the walls of a city. With the coming of firearms, the days of knights in armor were numbered; a well-aimed bullet could penetrate or damage the best armor of the Medieval period. The entire concept of war changed. It changed not only in battle strategy, but also in the preparation for war; a nation now needed an involved industry to produce gunpowder and the weapons that used it.

What changes came about as the result of the invention of gunpowder?

The advent of guns also broke down the feudal system. A robber baron felt secure when protected by his many men, but as guns began to find their way into the hands of the common folk, a trend toward more equality between peoples began to make itself felt.

Gunpowder, as used in firearms, also made possible the exploration and colonization of the New World. In the year 1003, a viking expedition under Thorfinn Karselfni came to colonize the New World. They landed somewhere on the New England coast and settled down to farm the land. They did not last long. Within three years, the outnumbered colonists were beaten off by the Indians and the few survivors returned to their homeland. If the vikings had been equipped with rifles, they might have established an empire in the New World like the empire that was established by the Spanish, who began their invasion after the Columbus expedition of 1492. Throughout the succeeding century, Spanish captains like Cortez and Pizzaro succeeded in firmly implanting a Spanish domain in the Americas. They were followed by the Dutch and the English. Although these groups were just as outnumbered as the vikings, they had an advantage. It was later in history and they possessed firearms, weapons that both intimidated and defeated the primitively equipped inhabitants of the New World. Since then, gunpowder-loaded weapons have been an important part of every exploring and colonizing expedition. Without them, the spread of the Europeans throughout the New World might have been impossible.

But gunpowder brought with it another, and more peaceful, occupation. It became an industrial explosive, thus serving a valuable function in mining and excavation. It was used also to blast rocks apart, so creating a greater supply of stones for building materials. Although later supplanted by nitro-glycerine and dynamite, gunpowder was the first industrial device that allowed men to move and clear away huge masses of rock and earth.

Not yet, but the time is not far off when

Has gunpowder outlived its usefulness?

other devices that can release large amounts of energy instantaneously will replace this ancient compound. Scientists are now working on different methods of propelling bullets and shells. Compressed gases, electricity, and atomic energy may some day produce propellant energy as easily but more efficiently than gunpowder. Rocket fuel, in some applications, is already replacing the explosive powder. Modern industry already has many different types of explosives, some of which do not resemble gunpowder at all, that perform the mining and land-clearing tasks with greater efficiency and more safety.

But gunpowder was the basic invention, a way to store explosive energy in a small package, a concept, brand-new in its time, that sprang from the mind of man and that gave him power his muscles could never attain.

Printing

When Johannes Gutenberg used movable type to print the first book in history, he ended an era that had started thousands of years before his time, and began another that still exists.

The concept of preserving ideas, events, and history is an invention of humanity as a whole, and the beginnings of this concept appeared quite early in man's time on earth. Some 20,000 years ago, a period labeled by scientists as the Late Paleolithic Era, men inscribed scenes on the walls of caves. These paintings described hunting incidents, battles between tribes, and also showed the tools and weapons used by those early men. In these caves, which have been found in France, Spain, and Africa, are the first permanent records of man's life during that most primitive era. The pictures help us to understand this part of man's history, and demonstrate man's desire to record his doings. But having no alphabet, they were not a form of writing, only colored pictures on cave walls.

Actual writing took a long time to develop. For thousands of years, men inscribed their happenings and sent their messages in the form

When did writing begin?

of pictures which represented the events. They were known as "pictographs" and not until about 3500 B.C. did this system begin to develop into a system of writing.

Archaeologists have determined that the earliest form of writing was born in Erech, a city of the Sumerians which flourished around 3500 B.C. Within its ancient ruins, they discovered hundreds of clay tablets, all inscribed with symbols, pictures, and number markings. This, they believe, was the first time in man's long history that a method of writing appeared. The Sumerian inscriptions used some pictures, but they were surrounded with other markings and signs that denoted sounds and monetary amounts. It was a step above the pictograph. Some of the marks actually represented verbal expression, and some combinations actually formed words.

The Egyptians and the Orientals kept the pure pictograph method for a much longer period but in Sumer, man made another step from barbarism to civilization with the invention of writing.

It is now generally believed that the first use of writing was for keeping lists at temples of worship. In many of the ancient kingdoms, the priestly hierarchy was very powerful and they collected a yearly

How was writing first used?

The earliest means of communication between primitive men was doubtlessly the sign language.

While many primitives used pebbles as counters (right), the Peruvian Incas used knotted ropes.

The simple drawing at right is a pictograph; the touching message left by a starving Eskimo shows a man in a boat, a tent, a man with outstretched arms, and a man with his hand to his mouth. It reads: "I went out in my *kayak*, pitched my tent, and had nothing (the outstretched hands) to eat."

The Egyptian hieroglyphic writing was a puzzle for quite some time. While the vocalization of the Egyptian language is still unknown, the meaning of the signs was discovered in 1822. During Napoleon's campaign in Egypt in 1799, a stone slab was unearthed which became known as the Rosetta Stone, after the name of the town where it was found. Three kinds of writing were carved on the slab: Greek, hieroglyphic, and another kind nobody recognized. This

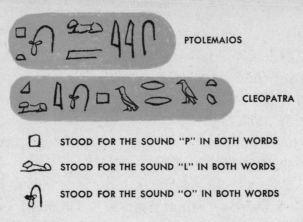

PTOLEMAIOS

CLEOPATRA

STOOD FOR THE SOUND "P" IN BOTH WORDS

STOOD FOR THE SOUND "L" IN BOTH WORDS

STOOD FOR THE SOUND "O" IN BOTH WORDS

third kind was later called "Demotic writing." After years of classifying and comparing, at last in 1822, the Frenchman Champollion succeeded in deciphering the hieroglyphics. His last clue was the name of the Egyptian King Ptolemy (Ptolemaios) which appeared in Greek on the Rosetta Stone. He compared the Greek signs with the corresponding Demotic signs and the hieroglyphics, or at least what he thought was the name in hieroglyphics. From this comparison, he deducted the shapes of the hieroglyphics corresponding with the Greek sounds. He then wrote in hieroglyphics how he thought the name of Cleopatra would have to be written. When, later, the name of Queen Cleopatra was discovered in hieroglyphic writing written exactly as he had predicted, he had proof that his key was correct. At right, we give in hieroglyphics the names of Cleopatra and Ptolemy and some of Champollion's clues.

Sumerian cuneiform writing on a fire-baked clay tablet.

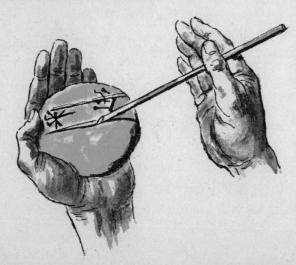

The receipt given by the Egyptian tax collectors to the farmers was a notation written in hieroglyphics on the wall of the farmer's building.

The Sumerians made their signs with a wedge-shaped stylus on a soft clay tablet. The signs are known as "cuneiform writing" from the word cunei, meaning "wedge." When the tablet was firebaked, the writing was more durable than today's pencil- or ink-marks.

tribute from all the subjects of the realm. In order to keep track of the thousands of items taken from the people year after year, clay tablets were inscribed with lists of the tribute.

The other early use of writing was by merchants. Many of the tablets found in the ruins of the Sumerian Empire contain lists of produce and items for sale. Some are bills!

This was the beginning. It would be a long time before man would use his newly found skill for setting down ideas, in addition to business lists.

Once men found that they could make

What were the next steps in the development of writing?
marks to signify syllables and sounds, there was no longer a need to draw pictures. Gradually, the pictographs changed into pure symbols. By 3000 B.C., the Sumerians, the Hittites, the Babylonians, and the Assyrians developed cuneiform writing, a system of wedge-shaped marks impressed in clay that was able to completely express the various languages.

Time went on. Thousands of years passed and slowly the cuneiform system replaced pictographs completely, but it, too, was doomed. By 1700 B.C., the Minoan Empire had developed an actual script. Gone were the wedge-shaped figures; people began to write in flowing curves. Freed from the restriction of straight lines, the scope of writing expanded to express much more. But it still represented only items and ideas and, at the best, a few syllables. An alphabet was needed. It ar-

rived a thousand years after the onset of the Minoan script, and it began a whole new era.

Archaeologists have determined that

Who invented the alphabet?
the first workable alphabet was Phoenician in origin and written as a crude script. However, each letter stood for a sound and had a symbol of its own. This alphabet, dating from 1600 B.C., is the ancestor of all modern Western alphabets. Once introduced, it spread rapidly through the Middle East and, finally, people of the time were able to write out complete words. Ideas could be expressed much more easily than before, and narrative stories and poetry began to appear.

The first Greek alphabet was developed from the Phoenician some time during the fifth century B.C. It was changed, improved, and extended until it had great flexibility. It became known as the Ionic alphabet and had 24 characters. When the Romans smashed the Greek Empire, they adopted this alphabet and adapted it to their own needs. In so doing, they gave us most of our modern languages. Their language was Latin, the basis for most of the Western tongues, and the actual shapes of the letters we use in print today are descended from the shapes of the early Roman letters.

Throughout the succeeding centuries, many people learned to use this alphabet. As the European continent slowly divided into separate countries, these areas developed their own languages. Some varied the alphabet or made their own, changing the shapes of the letters, but the majority of languages were either offshoots of Latin or influenced by it to the extent of using the familiar Roman alphabet.

Then, writing came to another standstill. The alphabet had been formalized, standard shapes for all the letters had been adopted, and that was it. With the fall of Rome in the fifth century and the onset of the Dark Ages, most of the world was illiterate. The art of writing was confined to monks, scholars, and some businessmen. Since all writing had to be done by hand, the making of copies was a long and difficult task and a handwritten book was quite expensive. Learning to read was a luxury because it was so difficult to obtain reading material.

A new invention was needed — not a change in the system of writing — but a way to make many copies easily and cheaply. It came, perhaps much later than it should have, but when it came, it unalterably changed the course of human history. The date was 1440 and it marked man's first use of movable type.

Before the mid-1450's, printing was accomplished **What is movable type?** by carving all the letters for an entire page onto a large wooden block, inking the face, and squeezing the block onto a piece of

When about 2000 B.C. the Seirites, a Semitic people, used 22 Egyptian ideographs to represent the sounds of their own language, the use of this innovation spread fast and was carried abroad, especially by the Phoenician traders. When the Greeks applied the symbols to the sounds of their language, they added symbols for the vowels.

| PHOENICIAN | OLD HEBREW | GREEK | ROMAN |

During the dark Middle Ages, the monks preserved the learning of the Western World by copying Greek and Roman manuscripts by hand.

paper in a machine that resembled a wine press. It was a difficult and painstaking process. Skilled woodworkers had to carve each individual letter in its exact place, a job that consumed a great deal of time. Because of the difficulty in preparing the blocks, the only kind of printing done then was for titles and decoration. The rest of the book was usually handwritten.

With the revolutionary invention of movable type, each letter was an individual block of type which could be inserted into a frame along with the other letters. It was not a new idea in the 1400's. Marco Polo, in 1298, told about the Chinese method of printing with individual blocks of type; Chinese researchers date this practice as far back as the 11th century. During that century, a Chinese craftsman named Pi Sheng made individual letters of baked earthenware and set them in a block of wax which he inked and pressed onto paper. By 1300, the Chinese were using

wood blocks. The Koreans outdid them by making letters with metal.

Yet, despite this evidence, the invention of printing with movable type is

Who was the European inventor of printing?

regarded as a European discovery of the 15th century and ascribed to Johannes Gutenberg, a printer of Mainz, Germany.

Although the Orientals were really first with the discovery of the movable-type printing process, it was actually the Europeans who developed the idea, started it on the road to perfection and, in so doing, created an industry.

There is still some mystery connected with this invention. Four names are mentioned whenever the discovery of printing is discussed. They are Johannes Gutenberg, Lourens Coster, Peter Schöffer, and Johannes Fust. Historians did not agree for a long time on all the

facts and theories, but in an effort to settle the dispute they decided to call Johannes Gutenberg the inventor of movable type since his life was the best documented.

Gutenberg, born around 1400 in Mainz, was a printer who worked very diligently at his task of cutting letters into wooden blocks. At some time during the 1400's, he conceived the idea of casting each letter as a small block of metal. No one knows whether he had heard of the Chinese and Korean systems, or if he took the idea from the Dutch printer, Lourens Coster, who may or may not have thought of the same method earlier. At any rate, Gutenberg was financed by Johannes Fust and his son-in-law, Peter Schöffer, who were also printers and metal-casters. Because of this close association, the facts are hazy. At one time, the experts advanced all the names as the actual inventors.

What was the Gutenberg process? Once Gutenberg decided to make metal type, he began to search for the right metal. He started with brass, which he melted and poured into sand molds that had the

HAND-OPERATED
PRESSES FOR
MOVABLE TYPE

MOVABLE TYPE

At left, Gutenberg's workshop; above, three old printing presses; and at right, two samples of early movable type.

shapes of the letters. But brass was too soft; it would not stand the pressure of printing for long. Gutenberg looked further. He finally settled on a mixture of lead and tin, an alloy that is easy to melt and cast, but which stubbornly retains its shape under pressure.

Gutenberg also found that sand molds were not accurate and devised a method of making metal molds. First, the letter was carefully cut, shaped, and polished on the end of a copper or iron rod. Next, this was hammered into a soft metal, probably lead, where it left a negative impression. Then, the alloy for the type itself was melted and poured into the mold. However, this was not the entire invention. Gutenberg also designed a tray into which the individual letters were assembled as words and clamped into place. The tray was set into a hand press, inked, and squeezed down on the sheet of paper. We can see that Gutenberg did not invent just a method of making movable type. He devised the entire process of printing from the typecasting and the mixing of the ink to the final steps of typesetting and stamping.

Like all other basic inventions, it was revolutionary. Many copies could be made in a short time and then the same type could be removed and reassembled for another printing.

There are disputes about the exact date of the first book but, **What were the first books to be printed in this way?** contrary to popular opinion, the famous Gutenberg Bible was not the first. A calendar and some poetry were printed around 1448 and a book on speechmaking appeared in 1450. The famous Bible was produced in 1454 in an edition of 300 copies although only 47 remain in existence today.

This was the beginning. Other printers soon adopted the Gutenberg system and books began to flood the world of the late 1400's. At the same time, other inventors were designing more efficient methods of casting type, mixing ink, making paper, and improving the presses themselves. The challenge was to make them entirely of metal and then to have them feed the paper automatically. In the 16th century, Leonardo da Vinci, the Italian artist and genius of science who painted the Mona Lisa, described a way to move the paper horizontally and the press vertically so that printing could be done in one operation. From that time on, development was rapid.

Today, our presses are completely automatic. Linotype machines cast entire lines of type in one piece while the operator types the words on the keyboard, and photographic processes are used to make plates for printing. Amazingly complicated machines can now print an entire newspaper, put it together, and fold it — all in one continuous operation.

Printing was as important to the social **What did the invention of printing mean to man?** and cultural development of man as the wheel was to his technology. With books and papers easy to make in large quantities, more and more people learned to read. With reading came knowledge, and with knowledge, a desire for freedom from tyrannical political systems. Printing started a world ferment that has never ended. The newspaper, an outgrowth of the invention of printing, was one of the most important forces in freeing man from serfdom and tyranny. In modern times, one of the first things a dictator-run country does is to destroy books, and rigidly control the reading material available to its people.

Books are among the most valuable possessions of humanity. They contain its history, its ideas, its religions and philosophies, and they provide a historic sense of continuity. In a modern library, one can cover the entire history of man; learn his achievements, his hopes, and his accumulated knowledge. Books preserve for future generations the experiences of the past, provide school children a means of studying, scholars a way to research, and give all of us enjoyment and relaxation when we read for pleasure.

It was inevitable that inventive man should find some method of recording himself. The development of printing was that method.

Optics

Our eyes are most marvelous optical instruments. Indeed, vision has been called the most valuable of our senses. The ability to see and appreciate the world around us is perhaps the most exciting experience given to us through our senses.

Our eyes are intricately constructed. They have an accurate and flexible lens suspended on a network of muscles which can change the curvature of the lens so that we can focus on objects at varying distances. This lens is so fine that it can, by a change of shape, focus from several inches to infinity. In front of the lens is the iris which has a central opening, the pupil. Also by means of muscular control, the iris opens and

EARLY LENS GRINDER

closes to regulate the amount of light striking the lens. At the back of the eyeball is the retina which, like a screen, receives a sharply focused image and transmits it to the brain.

This delicate and precise organ gives us sight, yet man has sought to go beyond its capabilities. He wanted to see details at a great distance, to peer into the minute world of microscopic creatures, and to record permanently those

Droplets of water form natural magnifying lenses.

things which his eyes could see but not preserve. The key to this extension of man's eyesight was the manufactured lens. Man copied nature, perhaps unwittingly, and learned to build lenses himself. At the same time, he inaugurated the science of optics, which is the study of light, its properties, and the means to control it.

It seems likely that the principle of the

Were lenses invented or discovered?

curved lens was discovered through observation. Droplets of water form natural lenses, and if one studies a drop of water on a leaf, one will find that the surface of the leaf is magnified. Although the principle of the lens was probably found through observation, the artificial lens itself was invented. It was not invented deliberately but came about through accident, trial and error, and the gradual accumulation of knowledge. No single man invented the lens.

The requirements for a lens are a transparent substance in which the thickness can be regulated and that can be shaped to a desired curve. Lenses could not be made until glass was invented. Glass fits the requirements exactly. The first glass objects in history were made in Mesopotamia and Egypt in 2500 B.C. It is obvious that keen-eyed observers of the time must have noticed that strange things happen to rays of light when they pass through variously shaped pieces of glass. Yet, the concept of using curved glass for lenses did not come for many centuries. What had to be understood was that when the curvature is controlled and balanced against the thickness, this combination bends light. This bending, or refraction, results in magnification.

One of the first men to discuss this phenomenon scientifically was the Greek, Ptolemy. His book, *Optics,* written in the second century, describes the bending of light by glass globes filled with water. In the 11th century, the Islamic scientist Ibn al Haitham, known as Alhazan, wrote a much more detailed book covering the reflection of mirrors and the magnification possible with curved segments of glass.

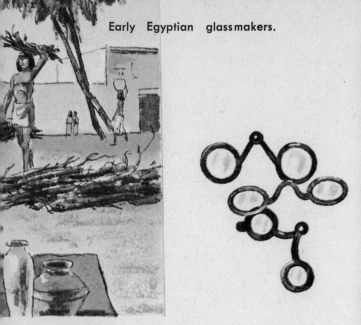
Early Egyptian glassmakers.

The first known portrait of a man with spectacles was painted in Italy in 1352 by Tommaso di Barisino.

Yet all of this early work was only theoretical. No one had attempted to use this bending of light for practical purposes and, for many years, the phenomenon remained a curiosity. It wasn't until the 13th century that serious experimentation began although many men could grind lenses by then.

The first practical use of a glass lens

What was the practical use of the lens?

was not in a telescope, not in a microscope, but in eyeglasses! This came about as the result of the work of two Englishmen in the 13th century. The Bishop of Lincoln, Robert Grosseteste, realized that lenses would not only magnify tiny objects, but would also make distant things seem to be closer. His experiments with this concept led his pupil, Roger Bacon, to start research into the problems of improving defective vision with external lenses.

Although Grosseteste and Bacon began the basic research on eyeglasses, no one knows the name of the man who made the first working pair of spec-

tacles. They appeared in Venice toward the end of the 13th century. Historians believe that the invention itself was made in 1286, but there are no other facts available. Venice was the center of glass industry at that time, and it seems logical that lens manufacture would begin there also.

The early eyeglasses were crude instruments, equipped with simple convex lenses. It was not until the late 16th century that scientists learned enough about the function of the eye to realize that other lens shapes would also help defective vision.

The origin of the telescope is shrouded

Did Galileo invent the telescope?

in mystery. Galileo, the Italian mathematician and physicist, is credited as its inventor since he was the first man to make important astronomical observations with the instrument.

Galileo, however, was not the original designer of the telescope. The Dutch were the first to use the instrument. The diary of Johannes Janssen describes the achievements of his father, Zacharias, a spectacle-maker. About 1590, the elder Janssen discovered that a combination of a convex lens with a concave lens for an eyepiece enabled its user to see distant objects not only more clearly, but with greater magnification — a discovery that became known in history as the principle of the compound microscope.

In 1608, Hans Lippershey, a Dutch optician, made use of this new knowledge to devise a telescope. The instrument was immediately adopted for military use. However, Lippershey did not invent this wonderful tool for seeing at great distances. His discovery was made because he had inspected an earlier telescope, one made in Italy. No one knows who the Italian designer was, but the instrument itself had the inscribed date, 1590. In addition, no one knows if this telescope was the first of its kind or a development of an even earlier model. The Italians of that period did not use telescopes; no mention of the instrument appears in writings of the time. The mystery will probably never be solved.

Galileo built his telescope in 1609, admittedly based on his knowledge of the Dutch instrument. However, Galileo went much further. He was primarily interested in the telescope as a research tool and turned it toward the skies. It was Galileo who first saw the rings around the planet Saturn and the moons of Jupiter. These discoveries were so astounding in their time that Galileo became known as the inventor of the telescope, a misconception that persists even today.

How was the telescope improved? The improvement of the telescope to the powerful instrument of our time was a long gradual process involving many men and many centuries. It was all based on the improvement of lenses.

Galileo's telescope was quite simple. It had two lenses in a lead tube. In

Galileo first demonstrated his telescope in Venice.

GALILEO'S REFRACTING TELESCOPE

1610, Johannes Kepler of Germany advanced the art of optics by using a more complicated lens system which gave higher magnification. That was the beginning. From that time on, developments came rapidly and from many countries. As the 17th century moved on, other researchers began to work on lenses and lens combinations. Huygens, of Holland, learned to grind lenses that would focus more accurately and made some that brought the rays of the sun down to a flaming pinpoint.

Isaac Newton, the great English physicist, after spending much time in designing color-corrected lenses, made a great improvement on the astronomical telescope. There had been experimentation with curved mirrors that gathered the reflection of an image and focused it. Newton used this technique in what is now known as the reflecting telescope. The mirror received the distant image and sent it through a system of lenses for magnification. This device, the reflecting telescope, is the one we use today for most astronomical observation. The modern version is essentially the same as Newton's in principle.

In the telescope used by Huygens, the eyepiece and the objective were mounted separately without a connecting tube.

The reflecting telescope has the highest power and allows us to see distant galaxies — galaxies that are millions of light years away.

Present-day telescopes are precision machines with lenses and mirrors of special glass ground with extreme accuracy. These optical components are carefully mounted in huge motor-driven frames and tubes. The reflecting mirror in the telescope on Mount Palomar in

Schematic drawings of a refracting telescope (above) and a reflecting telescope (at right).

NEWTON'S REFLECTING TELESCOPE

California is 200 inches in diameter, a far cry from the crude lead tube of Galileo with its tiny lenses.

Although the telescope has been and is still a great aid for surface observation on the earth, it is in the study of the universe that it achieves its greatness as an invention.

What is the importance of the telescope?

Most of the knowledge that we now have about the planets of our solar system, our sun, other stars, comets, nebulae, galaxies — in fact, all of the bodies of the universe — came from the use of the telescope. In the study of the workings of the universe, we learned much about the history, composition, and development of the planet we live on.

But the telescope did more than just bring factual knowledge. It expanded man's thinking. The very idea of looking out into the immensity of space led man to realize that neither the earth nor the sun are the centers of the universe. He was able to place his position in the cosmos and to understand that the earth is but one part of a mighty system of stars, nebulae, and galaxies. The telescope changed the perspective of man in relation to his planet.

Some day, we shall install telescopes on the moon, and perhaps on Mars. There, without the fuzzy blanket of atmosphere that surrounds the earth, we'll be able to see the heavens more clearly and our vision will penetrate the void of space even more deeply.

The development of the microscope closely paralleled the growth of the telescope for a microscope is actually a telescope designed

Who invented the microscope?

The reflecting telescope is the type used most in our modern observatories, and the Hale telescope (at right) in the Mount Polomar Observatory in California is one of the most powerful. Above, the dome of Mount Polomar Observatory.

40

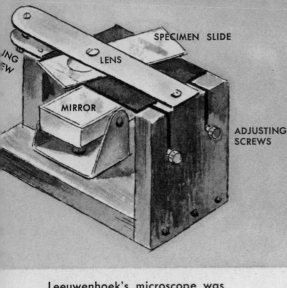

SPECIMEN SLIDE

LENS

MIRROR

ADJUSTING SCREWS

Leeuwenhoek's microscope was a simple instrument, but an important beginning.

The Englishman Robert Hooke, commissioned by the Royal Society, designed and built a practical compound microscope in 1664.

EYE

Schematic drawing of a simple microscope.

CONVEX LENS

OBJECT

IMAGE

to work at very short distances. The optical principles of both instruments are the same. Galileo made the first microscope, an adaptation of one of his telescopes. At the beginning, this use of lenses to look at tiny objects was an amusing hobby.

A Dutch dry-goods merchant and janitor, Anton van Leeuwenhoek, made this amusement a science. He made a hobby of grinding lenses, for he believed that no one else could make them as well as he. Leeuwenhoek worked all day in his store, and then spent long nights in his dusty basement grinding and polishing his lenses. He worked for years, gradually perfecting his technique, and eventually learned to make lenses of extreme curvature that were only an eighth of an inch in diameter. He mounted these tiny polished bits of glass in silver or gold frames of his own manufacture.

Once he had mounted them, he proceeded to look into a world that had been far too small for the naked eye to see. Leeuwenhoek examined the pores of his skin, the wings of insects, the teeming life in a drop of water. He discovered how pure water becomes infested with microbes when allowed to stand in the open air and, in 1674, Anton van Leeuwenhoek became the first man in history to describe the red corpuscles of the blood.

Anton van Leeuwenhoek's microscopes opened another world for mankind. The telescopes turned man's eyes up and outward to the gigantic immensity of the universe. The microscope focused his attention downward into a world he never knew existed, a world crowded with minute life, a world that contained the source of many diseases that plagued his body.

41

The compound microscope shown here is also called a "biological microscope" and is of the type used in most laboratories today.

What science did the microscope revolutionize?

If the discovery of lenses and the development of the science of optics had done nothing more than give us the microscope, it would have been enough. The microscope is one of the most valuable inventions to ever come from the mind of man. Without it, medical science might still be struggling to find the causes and cures of many diseases.

It would take many pages to list the life-saving discoveries that were made with the aid of the microscope. The work of men like the German scientist Robert Koch, who isolated the bacillus of tuberculosis, Louis Pasteur, the Frenchman, the conqueror of rabies, and Jonas Salk, the American scientist who quite recently defeated polio, to name just a few, would never have been possible without this marvelous instrument that allows us to see things too small for our eyes to focus on.

The microscope has uses in many fields of endeavor. Chemists, physicists, biologists, metallurgists, and other scientists all use the microscope as a tool for research. In our time, it has developed beyond just the use of lenses. The electron microscope can probe even more deeply than the conventional one. Although it has no real lenses, its principle is like that of the ordinary microscope. With the electron microscope, it is possible to see the molecules and atoms that are the basic building blocks of all matter.

What was the first camera to use a lens?

Today, the photographic industry depends on lenses, mirrors, prisms, and other optical devices, but there was

Only a hundred years ago, taking a portrait photograph was still an exhausting task for model and photographer alike. Even in bright sunlight, the exposure time was minutes and not fractions of seconds, as it is today. To prevent the "victim" from moving, the head was held steady in a frame.

a time when cameras did not use lenses at all. The device was known as the *camera obscura*, which simply means a dark chamber, and that is just what it was. Alhazan described in the 11th century the principal of the *camera obscura* by which a tiny pinhole in the room refracted the light rays and projected an upside-down image on the far wall. The image, however, was neither sharp nor too bright.

In the 16th century, Geronimo Cardano, the Italian physician, mathematician, and astrologer, used a convex lens in a *camera obscura* and, in a sense, started the photographic industry. Of course, there was no way to make a permanent record of the image. The closest one could come to a photograph was to trace the image as it was projected on a piece of paper. Photography, as we know it, actually began in 1816 when Joseph Niepce, a French researcher, captured an image on paper that had been sensitized with silver chloride.

Cameras today depend completely on lenses — refined, elaborated, but essentially the same as the first lenses that projected an image. Television cameras also use lenses in the same way, focusing the image of an actor onto an electronic screen, and in the movies, the lenses of projectors hurl the pictures on the film across the auditorium to fill a huge screen.

The camera, of course, serves as much more than just a source of entertainment. Among its many uses is as a recorder of history. Just as the cave paintings of the prehistoric men tell us about their life, the photography which began in the 19th century will inform the people of the future about our own lives. Hundreds of years from now, they will be able to see just how we lived. They will see our famous men and the important events of our time. And due to the motion picture camera, which also records sound, they will see us move and hear us speak. The camera is now providing a family album of man — an album in color, sound, and movement.

Some of the many uses of lenses today.

It would take many pages to list the devices that use **To what other uses have lenses been put?** lenses in our world today. Every device that controls light has a lens or other optical item in it somewhere. Solar batteries use lenses to concentrate the light of the sun into the electronic cell, and instruments with tiny dials are equipped with covering lenses to magnify the numbers. The flashlights we take camping, the powerful floodlights and spotlights used by the Navy, the stage lighting in a theatre, and automobile headlights all use lenses to direct the light in a focused beam.

The lensmakers have not forgotten the first use of this optical device, the humane job of correcting defective vision. Today, it is possible to design eyeglasses that can improve almost all kinds of poor eyesight. People who would have been considered almost blind centuries ago can now go about the world with excellent vision due to the use of lenses. The latest such application are eyeglasses known as contact lenses that fit right on the eyeball itself.

Of the many basic inventions that humanity has produced, the science of optics and its development of lenses is one of the very few that actually took one of man's senses and extended it in a way that was only a dream in the distant past.

Primitive man would have been astounded to learn that, some day, his descendants would be able to see for millions of miles. He would have been amazed at the minute world of the microscope, and would have called the camera pure magic. Undoubtedly, he would be frightened at what seems an almost mystical control of light. Primitive man must have, on a quiet afternoon in the far past, studied a droplet of water on a leaf. He must have seen the markings of that leaf magnified slightly and wondered about it, but he could never have foreseen that the droplet of water would become the basis for a great invention.

From Then Till Now

We have covered only the beginning of man's basic inventions. Century after century, technology increased, ideas grew, and men discovered more and more about the nature of the world. The great inventions that came about were often the result of the work of many men, the step-by-step accumulation of knowledge. Some took several centuries to reach a climax of development; others came in a few years as researchers aided each other in experimentation. We will mention only briefly a few of the basic inventions and discoveries, about which other books in this series will be written.

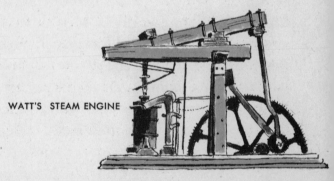

WATT'S STEAM ENGINE

The steam engine was mankind's first independent source of power. It freed man from his dependence on wind power for the sails of his boats or windmills, and he no longer had to depend on the water power of rushing rivers to turn the mill wheels. The steam

The steam engine

engine is ready to work any time a man wishes it to.

James Watt, the Scottish mathematical instrument-maker, designed the first workable steam engine in 1765. In the following century, it was developed as a stationary power source to operate machinery and as a mobile power source to run boats, cars, and trains.

The steam engine brought about a great industrial revolution in the Western world. It ran factories and, in trains, carried people across long distances with great ease. The world changed radically.

Electricity

Electricity is the most versatile force known to man. It runs our motors, lights our homes, and enables us to communicate over great distances. It has immense power, but it can be delicately and sensitively controlled.

The history of the development of electricity goes back to the ancient Greeks of 600 B.C., who first described the tiny sparks of static electricity that come from amber. In 1746, the Dutch researcher, Cunaeus, made the Leyden jar, the first man-made device that could store electricity. From that time on, the names of the many men who invented ways of generating, of storing, of transmitting, of making electricity do useful work are immortalized in the technical terms relating to that powerful force. *Ohms, watts, amperes, volts, henrys, farads* are some of the terms that describe the nature and operation of electrical forces. They are also the names of the men who discovered how to use those forces.

The internal combustion engine

In 1885, two Germans, Gottlieb Daimler and Karl Benz, designed an engine that burned a petroleum fuel and used the

The invention of the combustion engine started the "automobile age."

resulting power to generate motion. This was the internal-combustion engine, a power source that eventually replaced the steam engine as a method for running cars and trains.

This engine, as used in an automobile, was a revolutionary invention. The automobile provides personal transportation, transportation that is swift, comfortable; transportation that can take people great distances from city to city, country to country. Because of the automobile, men are no longer confined to their own areas as the men of the Dark Ages were.

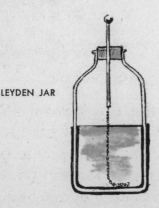

LEYDEN JAR

The internal-combustion engine is used for many other devices, too. It flies airplanes, runs boats, and powers lawnmowers. It is useful in hundreds of ways.

To be able to fly through the air like **Flight** the birds was a dream that haunted man all through his history. Every century had its experimenters, men who built cumbersome

THE "KITTY HAWK," THE WRIGHT BROTHERS' PLANE.

wings and tried to flap them like the birds. Many died in these experiments, but others kept on trying to imitate the flight of birds and failing each time.

In 1809, an English researcher, Sir George Cayley, changed the entire concept by pointing out that an aircraft must have rigid wings. This conclusion led to the work of the German, Otto von Lilienthal, who finally flew in a glider of his own design in 1891.

The next step was to provide such a glider with a power source. Experimentation moved to America, where Samuel Langley made several small models that were propeller-driven and powered with internal-combustion engines. Langley tried to make one large enough to carry a human being. It was unsuccessful although his small models flew beautifully.

The Wright brothers succeeded on December 17, 1903, when Orville Wright made the first successful powered flight in history. The air age began.

Our standard of living today is mainly **Mass production** the result of a technique by which we can make thousands of copies of the same items, all alike and with interchangeable parts. In earlier days, things were made individually by hand craftsmen. No two were exactly alike, and the prices were quite high.

For mass production to become a reality, several concepts had to be thought of — ideas, not machines. The first idea came early in the 19th century when an English engineer, Sir Joseph Whitworth, worked out a system of precise measurements. Until that time, measurements — like an inch, for example — were not standardized. But Whitworth invented methods to plot lengths, widths, thicknesses, etc., with extreme accuracy. This permitted the design of machine tools that could turn out uniform parts. Some years later,

MASS PRODUCTION

Samuel Colt applied this system to the production of his guns. All parts were interchangeable because they could be made with exact measurements.

Then, early in the 20th century, two

American automobile manufacturers completed the mass production process. Ransom E. Olds set up the first assembly line by having pre-produced parts delivered to his plant. Henry Ford then introduced the moving assembly line in which a car moved along the factory floor with component parts arriving at precise moments and at precise places. By the time the car reached the outer door, it was completely put together and ready to drive. Eventually Ford was able to turn out better than a car a minute!

Now, most items — appliances, even clothes — are produced cheaply and efficiently by this method.

Long-distance communication
For thousands of years, the only way to communicate over long distances was to send a messenger. But in the middle of the 19th century, the messenger began to be outmoded by faster and more reliable techniques. This came about because of the extreme flexibility of that useful force, electricity.

In 1844, Samuel F. B. Morse demonstrated his telegraph by sending the famous words, "What hath God wrought!" from Washington to Baltimore over a system of wires in his code system. In 1876, Alexander Graham Bell sent his voice over wires from one room to another on what we now call a telephone. The next step was communication without wires. Guglielmo Marconi made his first successful experiment with the technique of radio in Cornwall in the British Isles, sending signals, composed of minute amounts of

MORSE'S TELEGRAPH (RECEIVER)

electricity, through the air from Cornwall to St. John's, Newfoundland. Television, which sends actual pictures through the air, began with the invention of the iconoscope in 1928 by Vladimir Zworykin, a Russian-born scientist working in the United States.

Today, by radio, we can communicate all over the globe and with our satellites deep in space. The *Telstar* satellite, when perfected, will eventually enable us to send television images in full color to every part of the world.

HANDLING RADIOACTIVE MATERIAL

Atomic energy
When Albert Einstein perfected his mass-energy equation, $E = mc^2$, in 1905, he unlocked the secret of a new power source—atomic energy. In 1945, the first release of this energy as an explosion echoed over the deserts of New Mexico. A new era was born.

Although atomic energy gave mankind a fearful weapon of destruction, it also provided a peaceful power source.

In many countries in the world, atomic power stations now generate electricity. Atomic engines drive submarines and surface ships and may some day propel airplanes, cars, and rockets. It is the greatest power source ever discovered by inventive mankind.

Rockets and satellites

The ancient Chinese were the first to send a rocket into the air powered by an explosive mixture, but it was not until the mid-20th century that rockets became practical devices. Many men contributed to the development of this fastest of all vehicles. The Russian, Konstantin Tsiolkovsky, the German, Wernher von Braun, and the American, Robert Goddard, were all basic researchers in this exciting field.

Today, both the United States and the Soviet Union have perfected rockets to the point where they can leave the atmosphere of the earth and probe deep into space, exploring the mysteries of the moon and our neighboring planets. Some have carried men safely around the earth, and others have placed research satellites into stable orbits. This new invention, the rocket, has not only opened a whole new field of scientific study but has expanded man's exploratory horizons. Perhaps, and quite soon, men will land on the moon, on Mars, on Venus, and so pioneer another new era in the history of mankind.

Blast-off of a rocket. The invention of rockets made man's first attempts in the exploration of space and the beginning of the space age possible.